EASTERN NATIONAL

THE FINAL YEARS

DAVID MOTH

AMBERLEY

Seen in a very wet Chelmsford bus station on 27 January 1990 is one of the former United Counties Bristol VRTs that Eastern National purchased from Milton Keynes Citybus in 1986. This bus had the EN Citybus branding applied to vehicles employed on LRT tendered routes and it was unusual to see it this far from London. This bus passed in July 1990 to Thamesway, who withdrew it in January 1991. This bus was subsequently owned by Fords of Althorne and Emblings of Guyhirn, who sold it to a preservationist in 2016.

First published 2018

Amberley Publishing
The Hill, Stroud
Gloucestershire, GL5 4EP

www.amberley-books.com

Copyright © David Moth, 2018

The right of David Moth to be identified as
the Author of this work has been asserted in
accordance with the Copyrights, Designs and
Patents Act 1988.

ISBN 978 1 4456 7945 7 (print)
ISBN 978 1 4456 7946 4 (ebook)

British Library Cataloguing in Publication Data.
A catalogue record for this book is available from
the British Library.

Origination by Amberley Publishing.
Printed in the UK.

Introduction

This book is intended to be a collection of photographs taken by an amateur photographer during the period from April 1990, when Eastern National joined the Badgerline Group, up until the gradual disappearance of the Eastern National name and identity in the early years of the new century. This book is not intended to be seen as any kind of definitive history of the story of this much loved Essex operator, mainly for two reasons. Firstly, it would be presumptuous for me to attempt to do so, having never been employed in the bus industry. Secondly, I would probably inevitably get a lot of details wrong regarding depot closures, route changes and so on. That book will have to be written by someone else, and if and when that happens, I'll certainly look forward to reading it.

There is almost certainly a bias in the vehicle types represented in the images of this book, with Bristol VRTs in particular probably being over represented, while the number of pictures of minibuses and Leyland Nationals is less than their proportion of the fleet would probably merit. All I can say to that is that the VRTs, with their curvy ECW bodies betraying their NBC and indeed Tilling ancestry, were my favourite bus type, while minibuses were, to me, 'the enemy'.

The name Eastern National Omnibus Company Ltd was registered on 28 February 1929, although it wasn't until New Years Eve of that year that the National Omnibus & Transport Company Ltd and the London & North Eastern Railway were able to seal the agreement for the formation and working of the company.

In 1931 Thomas Tilling Ltd made a successful bid to the shareholders of the National Omnibus & Transport Company, which gave it control of its subsidiaries, including Eastern National. The Tilling Group was nationalised in 1948, and on 1 January 1969 all the former Tilling Group bus operating subsidiaries passed to the control of the newly formed state-owned National Bus Company.

For anyone interested in the history of Eastern National up until the formation of NBC I recommend the book *The Years Between 1930 to 1969* by R. J. Crawley, D. R. MacGregor and F. D. Simpson. For high-quality images of Eastern National buses up until 1969, I strongly recommend the excellent book *Glory Days: Eastern National* by Richard Delahoy.

Eastern National remained a subsidiary of the state-owned National Bus Company until 23 December 1986, when, as part of the privatisation process of NBC, Eastern National was purchased by a management buyout team. Eastern National was subsequently taken over by Badgerline Holdings on Maundy Thursday 12 April 1990. It is was by sheer coincidence that it was around this time that I bought my first 35 mm camera and started taking photographs of buses. Nevertheless, it does make a good starting date for this book.

The images in this book, all taken by myself, are arranged as much as is possible in chronological order, given that not every image has an exact recorded date. Hence, the photographs in this collection cover the gradual changing of the fleet under the ownership of Badgerline and subsequently First Group.

In July 1990 Eastern National's new owners partitioned their new acquisition, creating the new Badgerline Group subsidiary Thamesway, which took over operations at Southend, Hadleigh, Basildon, Brentwood and Ponders End depots. Eastern National retained operations at Bishops Stortford, Chelmsford, Great Dunmow, Braintree, Maldon, Colchester, Clacton and Harwich.

In a short space of time Thamesway set about transforming the majority of its fleet, replacing many of the traditional 'big buses' with minibuses. This rendered several Bristol VRTs surplus to requirements and these vehicles, with several useful years of life left in them, were transferred to the Badgerline fleet in the west of England.

Minibuses were gradually introduced onto the town routes in Chelmsford, a process that started in 1990 and was completed in 1993. 1993 also saw the introduction of a new livery, which was similar in design to the livery adopted for deregulation but in the colours of parent company Badgerline and controversially, along with other Badgerline-owned fleets throughout England and Wales, included a small stylised image of a badger behind the rear wheels.

In April 1995 Badgerline and GRT merged to create FirstBus (later First Group, then First). This led to the rapid removal of the badgers from the vehicles and the appearance of a 'Welcome to FirstBus' etching on the front nearside window of each vehicle. As the years went on the identities of the various subsidiaries of First gradually faded away. Eastern National and Thamesway were amalgamated again although vehicles retained the fleet names and colours for some years. The last buses to be delivered in Eastern National livery were a batch of P registration Dennis Lances with Northern Counties bodywork. First introduced two corporate liveries in 1998 – one for low-floor buses and the other for older 'step entrance' vehicles.

I believe the Eastern National name finally disappeared from the streets of Essex in 2002, although it was to make a brief re-appearance on two vehicles: a Dennis Dart new to Yorkshire Rider that was painted into a pseudo Tilling Green livery and the last surviving Bristol VRT, which was retained in semi-preservation by First Essex from October 2004 until it was sold for preservation in 2010.

I have tried to keep my captions as objective as I possibly can and have striven to be accurate. It is probably inevitable that the odd inaccuracy (or five) has crept in and for that I can only apologise. I hope you enjoy this collection.

David Moth
February 2018

Leyland National KCG 618L is seen at Chelmsford bus station in April 1990, shortly before Eastern National was taken over by Badgerline Holdings. This bus was new to Alder Valley.

Leyland Lynx 1413 (F413 MNO), photographed in Chelmsford some time in 1990.

A dull Maundy Thursday 12 April 1990 sees a couple of series 2 Bristol VRTs at Harwich Town. This was the day that Badgerline Holdings' takeover of Eastern National was completed.

Bristol VR series 2 JNO 190N is seen on 12 April 1990 at Harwich Town rail station. The last series 2 VRTs would be withdrawn within a year.

A dull Easter Sunday 15 April 1990 sees Dennis Dart demonstrator G541 JBV on loan to Eastern National. Eastern National's first Darts would arrive in 1993 under Badgerline ownership. The bus is seen calling at Chelmsford railway station.

East London Leyland Titan T109 (CUL 109V) and Eastern National Bristol VRT 3092 (STW 36W) are seen in April 1990, just after Eastern National had been taken over by Badgerline Holdings.

Unfortunately, it isn't possible to identify the Leyland Tiger in this image. This was taken during the part closure of Springfield Road in Chelmsford during the spring of 1990, hence the wooden fencing in the foreground of the image.

Leyland Olympians 4021 (C421 HJN) and 4017 (C417 HJN) are seen at Braintree bus park in April 1990.

Bristol VR KOO 787V and Ford Transit D751 RWC are seen in the summer of 1990.

In the summer of 1990, Leyland National MAR 786P and Bristol VRT XHK 216X are seen in Chelmsford High Street. It was fairly unusual to see a double-decker on the 56 by then and it would be converted to minibus operation soon after. The High Street was pedestrianised in 1993.

Bristol VRT 3083 (STW 27W) is seen on a summer's evening at the Heath Drive terminus of the 44A/B. This route was operated by double-deckers from the 1950s up until 1991. Eastern National were unique in that their VRTs were delivered new with seventy seats instead of the industry standard of seventy-four. This practise continued up until this batch, and their final two batches were of seventy-four-seaters. Eastern National acquired twenty-one VRTs from the Scottish Bus Group in exchange for Lodekkas in 1971 and 1973, and these were also downgraded to seventy seats.

Ford Transit D750 RWC is seen in Duke Street, Chelmsford, in July 1990. The 42 was introduced in October 1986 using Ford Transit minibuses running between Chelmsford bus station and Galleywood. It is now operated by full-sized buses and has subsequently been extended to Broomfield Hospital and Braintree, with the 42A offshoot running hourly to Stansted Airport.

Leyland Lynx 1407 (F407 LTW) is captured in Chelmsford bus station during the summer of 1990.

Bristol VRT 3111 (XHK 216X) is seen passing under the notorious railway bridge in Duke Street, Chelmsford, during the summer of 1990. The road surface here has recently been raised so not even low-height double-deckers can pass under it now.

Ford Transit C444 BHY, along with another unidentified Transit, is seen in Chelmsford bus station just having transferred from fellow Badgerline subsidiary Cityline and still to receive EN fleet names. Note this bus is still displaying Fishponds as its destination, a suburb of Bristol.

In 1990, open-top Bristol KSW WNO 479 was pressed into service as a driver trainer. She is seen on layover at Chelmsford bus station in the summer of that year.

Leyland National 2 STW 20W was allocated to Clacton by the time this photograph was taken. This bus spent her early years at Chelmsford and could often be seen on Chelmsford town services. This was numerically the last Leyland National purchased new by Eastern National, and is seen in Colchester bus station during the autumn of 1990.

Leyland National YEV 318S is seen on the cross Chelmsford 48 from Chelmer Village to North Melbourne during the autumn of 1990. Note the Morris Ital; they are about as common as hen's teeth now.

Leyland National 1811 (VNO 734S) is seen on Chignal Road, Chelmsford, during the autumn of 1990.

Bristol VRT BEP 963V and Ford Transit D752 RWC are photographed at Chelmsford bus station during the autumn of 1990. The VRT had just been transferred within the Badgerline Group from South Wales Transport. She would receive fleet number 3222 with Eastern National. Note the fixed glazing upper-deck front windows. Nationwide, more and more Bristol VRTs would receive these throughout the 1990s.

January 1991 sees Bristol VRT 3076 (KOO 794V) setting off from Chelmsford to Halstead on the long established 311, while 3093 (STW 37W) waits to join Duke Street on the cross Chelmsford 44B from Moulsham Lodge to North Melbourne.

Eastern National Bristol VRT CF3070 (KOO 788V) is captured at Chelmsford on 31 January 1991 while covering a diagram normally worked by a Ford Transit. Sadly, 3070 met a premature end in 1994 when she was stolen from the depot and the joyrider crashed her.

Eastern National Bristol VRT 3092 (STW 36W) is seen in Springfield Road, Chelmsford, in February 1991. This was an unusual working as the 55 was very much a Leyland National route and had been since 1978, when it was withdrawn between the bus station and Westlands Estate. It was extended at first to Havengore, then to New Bowers Way. The 55 was also extended from the bus station to North Melbourne in 1990, but that didn't last very long. Up until 1978 the 55 used to work between Westlands Estate and Boswells School and was entirely worked by Bristol FLFs. The 55 was eventually supplemented and replaced by the 54.

Eastern National Leyland Olympian Coach CR4503 (B691 BPU) is seen in Chelmsford High Street in early 1991. These long-wheelbase Olympians were the mainstay of the 53 between Chelmsford and Colchester (and the 71, its successor) for over a decade.

Bristol VRT 3111 (XHK 216X) going down Chelmsford High Street on the 44B, which had been scheduled for double deck operation since the 1950s. However, that came to an end later in that year as reductions of the double-decker allocation at Chelmsford depot led to Leyland Nationals taking over the 44A/B. This scene has changed tremendously as the High Street was pedestrianised a few years later and this location is now called Half Moon Square, the creation of which involved the controversial cutting down of trees.

Bristol VRT 3077 (STW 21W) sits at the Wicklow Avenue terminus of Melbourne Farm Estate, waiting to return to Moulsham Lodge via the town centre on the 44A.

An overcast 12 March 1991 sees Bristol VRT 3058 (LJN 653P) and Leyland Lynx 1426 (F426 MJN) at Chelmsford bus station.

Seen in Broomfield Road in March 1991 is Leyland Olympian C711 GEV on either the 44A or 44B. This bus-seated Olympian was based at Chelmsford, although during the cricket season she would often be temporarily based at the depot of the town where Essex County Cricket Club were playing their 'home matches' that week.

Leyland Lynx 1427 (F427 MJN) is captured on Barnard Road, Galleywood, on 17 April 1991. Eastern National purchased thirty Lynxes in 1988. The first two had E registrations and were delivered before the remaining twenty-eight to enable driver familiarisation to take place. The others were F registrations. They were fast vehicles although they were prone to rattles and a loud whine from the rear axle, which got worse with age.

Also seen on 17 April 1991 is Leyland Olympian 4020 (C420 HJN), which stands in Braintree bus park on the cross Essex 132 service from Colchester to Bishops Stortford. This was a variant of the 133. The western section of the route between Braintree and Bishops Stortford was abandoned by Eastern National some time ago. The present 133 from Braintree to Stansted Airport has passed through quite a few different operators over the years and has been operated by Network Colchester (now Arriva) since 2010. The section between Braintree and Colchester reverted back to its traditional number 70 and was extended to Chelmsford in 2009.

In July 1990 the Badgerline Group portioned Eastern National and the depots in Southend, Hadleigh, Basildon, Brentwood and Ponders End passed to new Badgerline subsidiary Thamesway. Major service revisions in the Southend area in January 1991 by Thamesway rendered several Bristol VRTs surplus to requirements. Ten of these vehicles, which still had years of useful life left in them, were transferred within the Badgerline Group to Badgerline itself. 25 April 1991 sees former Eastern National/Thamesway 3082 (STW 26W) in service in Bath with her new owner, now numbered 5550. This was the newest of the ten and the only W registration.

Also seen in Bath on 25 April 1991 is former 3074 (KOO 794V), looking every inch a native Badgerline bus despite her Essex heritage. These also differed from the native Badgerline VRTs in only having seventy seats instead of seventy-four.

Bristol VRT 3109 (UAR 599W) is seen in Chelmsford High Street on the 91 to Heybridge Basin via Hatfield Peverel and Nounsley. As this was a duty worked by Maldon depot, this Harwich-based bus must have been on loan to Maldon depot at the time. This VR had a bit of a nomadic existence with EN, being based at various times at Clacton, Harwich, Colchester, Braintree, and eventually with Thamesway.

Bristol VRTs 3054 (LJN 649P) and 3079 (STW 23W) are seen on layover at Maldon bus station on 1 May 1991. 3054 was withdrawn about a year after I took this photograph, but 3079 would have a long life with Eastern National, lasting into the twenty-first century.

Eastern National Bristol VRT 3094 (STW 38W) and Thamesway Leyland Olympian 4001 (XHK 236X) are seen in Chelmsford bus station on Saturday 13 July 1991. The Olympian was one of a batch of three received in 1981 and allocated to Southend. They passed to Thamesway upon the partition of 1990 and were later transferred within the First Group to Eastern Counties. It was quite rare to see a Thamesway double-decker in Chelmsford at this time, as the routes operated to Chelmsford by Thamesway (the 11, 351 and 152–4) were usually operated by Leyland Nationals.

An interesting gaggle of different bus types is seen at Chelmsford bus station on Saturday 13 July 1991, including Thamesway Leyland Olympian 4001 (XHK 236X) and unidentified Eastern National buses, including a Leyland National, a Bristol VRT and a Leyland Olympian coach.

Bristol VRT 3054 (LJN 649P), freshly repainted and looking superb even though she was nearing the end of her life with EN, is seen in Chelmsford High Street in July 1991 on the Essex County Council contracted route to Heybridge Basin. The LJN ...P batch had Leyland 501 engines.

Thamesway Leyland Lynx 1423 (F423 MJN) is seen in Chelmsford in July 1991 still in EN livery. It was almost a year before a Lynx would receive Thamesway livery. The 154 didn't normally run along this road so it must have been on a diversion. Thamesway normally used Leyland Nationals on their share of the 152/3/4 service, which was worked from their Basildon depot jointly with Eastern National's Chelmsford depot. The only other route that was worked jointly by the sister companies at the time was the 350/1 between Chelmsford and Romford.

Looking resplendent while basking in the summer sunshine at Heybridge Basin is Bristol VRT 3054 (LJN 649P) on Wednesday 31 July 1991.

This photograph of Bristol VRT 3112 (XHK 217X) was taken in Watchouse Road, Galleywood, on 1 August 1991. This bus would have a long career in Essex. Eastern National's successors First Essex withdrew her in 2003. She was sold on to RTF Commercials of Braintree, who re-registered her XIL 1254, before she was passed on to Flagfinders of Braintree, where she was used a lot on school services. She was then sold on in 2008, passing briefly through the ownership of Totally Transport of Blackpool and K&J Logistics of Rufforth. She was scrapped in 2009.

Bristol VRT 3070 (KOO 788V) stands in Barnard Road, Galleywood, on 1 August 1991. This bus received a very top-heavy version of EN's deregulation livery before receiving this final version.

Leyland Lynx 1408 (F408 LTW) is seen on 1 August 1991. As the only vehicle based at the now closed Great Dunmow outstation at the time, this vehicle did the same diagram almost every day, which involved working the 33 into Chelmsford and the 41A/B between Chelmsford bus station and Great Baddow.

Bristol VRT 3091 (STW 35W) is seen on 1 August 1991 in West Mersea.

In August 1991, Bristol VRT 3093 (STW 37W) is seen in a strangely quiet Duke Street, passing by Chelmsford railway station, which had been completely rebuilt in 1987/8. It wasn't too uncommon to see a VR on the 41A/B at the time.

Leyland Lynx 1427 (F427 MJN) is seen in Chelmsford in July 1991. At the time it was still rare to see a single-decker on the 44A/B during the daytime; they were worked by VRTs and Olympians during the day, with Lynxes taking over these routes in the evenings. This photograph was taken quite early in the morning, as can be seen by the direction of the shadows.

Bristol VRT 3079 (STW 23W) is seen pulling away from All Saints Church in Maldon on 15 August 1991.

Bristol VRT 3079 (STW 23 W) is seen waiting to depart Maldon bus station on a lunchtime run on the long established 31 to Chelmsford on Thursday 15 August 1991. Maldon bus depot/station was closed in 1993 and the 31 was extended from Maldon to Burnham-on-Crouch. Most services now on the 31 are operated as the 31B/X and go via Great Baddow bypass, therefore shaving several minutes off this long journey. Evening services are operated as the 31 and go through Great Baddow.

Bristol VRT 3060 (LJN 655P) drops off a passenger on Springfield Road, Chelmsford, on 15 August 1991 while working the 92 from Maldon to Chelmsford via Hatfield Peverel. This Leyland-engined VR would be gone from EN along with all the other members of the LJN-P batch within the next year or so. The 91/2 was an Essex County Council contracted service, which replaced the 38 upon deregulation. It was replaced by the 73 in April 1995.

Coach-bodied long-wheelbase Leyland Olympian 4503 (B691 BPU) is seen heading past the now closed Three Cups Public House on Springfield Road in Chelmsford. This pub used to attract people from all over Chelmsford, mainly due to its large pool hall at the rear of the pub. This building has seen further life as various different restaurants over the years since I took this photograph in October 1986.

Thamesway Leyland Olympian 4010 (C410 HJN) is seen at Southend bus station on Friday 16 August 1991. It is departing on the lengthy and long established famous 251, which had been operated since 1928 by Westcliff, then from 1955 by Eastern National after the absorption of Westcliff by EN, passing to Thamesway when EN was partitioned in July 1990. The 251 was curtailed at Walthamstow on 13 June 1981. Dwindling passenger numbers led to the eventual demise of the 251 on 6 May 2000.

Also at Southend bus station, this time on Wednesday 21 August 1991, Thamesway Leyland Olympian 4009 (C409 HJN) is also working the 251 to Walthamstow. These Olympians had coach seats from new and for that reason were very suited for this long route.

Leyland-engined Bristol VRT 3054 (LJN 649P) is seen outside the Coral Bingo in Moulsham Street, Chelmsford, on 11 October 1991 on the 36 to South Woodham Ferrers, having acquired more adverts since we last saw her on 31 July. This part of Moulsham Street was pedestrianised in 1993 as part of the High Street redevelopment.

Bristol VRT 3092 (STW 36W) is seen in Chelmsford High Street on 11 October 1991. This area has been absolutely transformed since I took this photograph.

19 November was a miserable, wet day. On that day, Thamesway Bristol VRT 3110 (XHK 215X) was at Walthamstow bus station, working the LRT tendered route 275. Unfortunately, I only ever seemed to photograph Thamesway VRTs in dull weather. Not many Bristol VRTs were remaining with Thamesway by then.

Leyland Lynx (F407 LTW) is captured in Galleywood on the 41B Chelmsford town service on Monday 23 December 1991.

Thamesway Leyland National 1866 (YEV 324S) is seen at Basildon bus station on 7 February 1992. I do regret not taking a photograph of this bus when I saw it in Blackburn one evening in the summer of 1996 after its conversion by East Lancs into a National Greenway.

Bristol VRT 3095 (UAR 585W) is seen on 10 February 1992. This bus was sadly lost in the arson attack at Colchester depot on Christmas Eve 1994.

Thamesway Leyland Lynx 1424 (F424 MJN) stands on layover at Romford railway station in the company of three East London Leyland Titans, waiting to return to Canvey Island on the long established 151 on Tuesday 25 February 1992.

Bristol VRT 3114 (XHK 219X) is captured at the roundabout near Colchester North railway station on Saturday 29 February 1992. In this image this location looks almost rural. The area was transformed not long after, with a huge retail complex and the roundabout being extensively remodelled.

Long-wheelbase Leyland Olympian 4501 (B689 BPU) is seen in March 1992. The 53 was a one of several long Eastern National routes that went right across the county; it once ran from Clacton to Tilbury Ferry. However, by the early 1970s it was reduced to just the section between Chelmsford and Colchester. Despite having what was nominally a Chelmsford area number, it was worked from Colchester depot for a long time. These long-wheelbase Olympian Coaches were the mainstay of the 53 for a long time. By the time I took this photograph, the NBC type fleet name had been replaced by the revised style for deregulation. Note the green EN bus stop, which was a familiar sight in most parts of Essex for a long time.

One of three Leyland Olympian Coaches with the revised 'Ebdon front' purchased by Eastern National in 1986 is seen in Springfield Road, Chelmsford, in 1992 on the 55 town service. Eastern National was the only operator to buy the low-height version of these Olympian Coaches. This vehicle had been used on EN's commuter coach services, but had recently been transferred to Colchester for use on the 53 when I took this photograph. Neither route exists now; the 53 was replaced in 1995 by the 71, which runs via Chelmer Village, and the 55 was supplemented and ultimately replaced by the 54. Incredibly, these three Olympians were the last double-deckers that were bought new by Eastern National.

Barely into her long journey on the 153 from Chelmsford to West Thurrock Lakeside via Billericay and Basildon, Leyland Lynx 1428 (F428 MJN) has just climbed Wood Street and is about to turn into Galleywood Road during the summer of 1992.

Sunday 19 April 1992 was a lovely, hot, sunny day. On that day Leyland Olympian 4013 (C413 HJN) and Bristol VRT 3084 (STW 28W) were basking in the warm Essex sunshine at Chelmsford depot behind the bus station. 4013 is in the dual-purpose version of EN's middle green and middle chrome yellow livery while 3084 is in the bus version.

Also seen on Sunday 19 April is Leyland Olympian 4011 (C411 HJN) in the revised dual-purpose livery. By this time a lot of the fleet were no longer carrying the metal plates denoting which depot they were placed at.

An interesting line up of double-deckers, consisting of Olympian 4013 and VRTs 3084, 3070, 3083 and 3077, are seen enjoying their day of rest at Chelmsford depot on Sunday 19 April 1992. It is interesting that 3084 has no depot plate, while the other four buses do. Also note that 3083 has the EN fleet name on the lower front dash panel, while none of the other VRTs in this image do.

Bristol VRT 3079 (STW 23 W) is looking very smart for an eleven-year-old bus on Milton Road, Maldon, on 28 May 1992. The batch received between October 1980 and February 1981 was the last batch of VRs delivered with seventy seats. EN received two further batches of VRs, which came with seventy-four seats.

Bristol VRT 3128 (XHK 233 X) is seen in Milton Road, Maldon, on 28 May 1992, with what appears to be a bus stop in someone's back garden.

Leyland Lynx 1429 (F429 MJN), numerically the last Leyland Lynx purchased new by EN in 1988, is seen behind Romford railway station on 6 June 1992, waiting to return to its home depot of Chelmsford on the long, inter-urban route 351. When EN was partitioned in 1990, sixteen Lynxes passed to Thamesway, with the balance of fourteen remaining with EN. The 351 was withdrawn between Brentwood and Romford in December 2005 and that section of the route was replaced by new TFL route 498.

Thamesway Leyland Lynx 1400 (E400 HWC) was the first Lynx to receive Thamesway livery. It had only just been applied when I took this photograph on Saturday 27 June 1992. It was sadly destroyed by fire in Romford in 2004.

Still in EN livery is 1412 (F412 MNO), which is seen having just arrived at Southend bus station after working in on the 2 from Basildon on 27 June 1992. By this time Thamesway and Southend Transport were locked in a fierce 'bus war'.

Coach-seated Olympian 4013 (C413 HJN) is seen nearing the end of its journey on the Chelmsford town service 41A in Watchouse Road, Galleywood, on 24 July 1992. This bus is in the dual-purpose version of EN's livery. It's curious how tall that bus stop seems to be.

Looking very smart in Eastern National's 'spinach and custard' deregulation livery is Bristol VR 3094 (STW 38W), which stands in Chelmsford bus station on 11 August 1992.

Seen in Chelmsford bus station in August 1992 is Leyland Olympian 4510 (D510 PPU), which is blinded for the commuter coach service 194.

Maldon-based Bristol VR 3127 (XHK 232X) is seen in Chelmsford bus station on layover, waiting to work the 92 to Maldon via Hatfield Peverel. It was obviously a hot day judging by the fact that all of the window ventilators are fully open.

Leyland Lynx 1427 (F427 MJN) is seen at Basildon Hospital on Friday 28 August 1992 on an early afternoon journey to its home depot of Chelmsford from West Thurrock Lakeside.

Bristol VR 3094 (STW 38W) is seen on 18 September 1992 at Maldon bus depot, which would be closed the following year. It's also interesting to note the advert for local Essex brewer Ridleys of Hartford End, who would be taken over by Greene King in 2005 and subsequently closed down.

This is the only photograph taken in Tiptree in this book. Maldon-based Leyland Lynx F425 MJN is seen on 18 September 1992 on the 119 to Clacton, although the working this bus is on terminates in Colchester.

There is something a little surreal about seeing a bus in Eastern National livery, displaying signs proclaiming it to be on loan to Eastern National. Thamesway Leyland Lynx 1410 (F410 MNO) is seen at Billericay railway station on Christmas Eve 1992.

By April 1993 more Lynxes had received Thamesway livery. 1411 (F411 MNO) is seen arriving in Chelmsford on the 154 from Lakeside. It was unusual for Basildon depot to put Lynxes out on this jointly operated route; Thamesway usually allocated Leyland Nationals to the 152/3/4.

Seen on layover, having worked in on the infrequent 31A from Chelmsford to Maldon via Little Baddow, is Leyland Lynx 1403 (F403 LTW), which stands in the soon to close Maldon bus station in April 1993.

Bristol VR 3128 (XHK 233X) is seen in New London Road in Chelmsford on 10 April 1993. The recent closure of the High Street resulted in buses now being routed along Tindal Street and New London Road, where they still operate to the present day.

A very smart looking Leyland National 2 1938 (STW 19W) is seen in Maldon depot on 10 April 1993, about to work the 119 to Clacton via Colchester. Maldon depot closed that spring.

Leyland National 2 1938 (STW 19W) looks very smart for a twelve-year-old bus. She is seen in Colchester on Saturday 10 April 1993. Shortly after this photograph was taken a new livery was introduced.

Seen on 21 March 1994, in the livery that was launched in the spring of 1993, is Leyland Olympian 4015 (C415 HJN). She is seen in the instantly recognisable Colchester bus station under the multi-storey car park, which was completed in 1972 and would be demolished not long after I took this photograph.

Leyland Olympian 4020 (C420 HJN) is also seen in the new livery in Coggeshall Road, Braintree, on 21 March 1994. The new livery was clearly inspired by the colours of parent company Badgerline. Indeed, it even included a small badger behind the rear axle, which was the Badgerline Group's subtle way of introducing a corporate identity to its subsidiaries. It also included a large 'E', which was intended to stand for several things, including Essex and East of England.

Leyland Lynx 1427 (F427 MJN) is seen in Coggeshall Road, Braintree, on 21 March 1994, still in the spinach and custard deregulation livery, on the 35 from Chelmsford to Halstead via Braintree. The direct route between Chelmsford and Braintree was part of the 311 for decades. However, since the early 1990s various service revisions have seen this route become part of the 43, the 35, the 350/1, the 352 and the 70. Now the direct route between Chelmsford and Braintree is served by overlapping sections of the 70 from Colchester to Chelmsford and the 42 from Galleywood to Braintree, although this does now mean that this route enjoys a bus every fifteen minutes during the daytime.

Bristol VRT 3218 (ONH 924V) is seen at Colchester bus station on 21 March 1994. This was one of nineteen VRTs new to United Counties that were purchased from Milton Keynes Citybus in 1986. Most of these vehicles passed to Thamesway and were sold on in 1991. By the time I took this photograph, 3218 was the last survivor of the nineteen with EN, its destination equipment having been modified during its time with EN. Sadly, this bus perished in the arson attack on Colchester bus depot of Christmas Eve 1994.

Also seen in Colchester on 21 March 1994 is Leyland National 1824 (VAR 901S). It seemed to be the case on this bus that the deregulation livery had been applied over the NBC symbol as the paint covering the sticker had worn away by the time I took this photograph. It was EN's policy at the time not to paint Leyland Nationals or Bristol VRTs into the new livery. This bus wasn't with EN for much longer and saw further service with Classic of Annfield Plain.

Bristol VRT 3109 (UAR 599W) is photographed resting at Harwich Town on 21 March 1994. Note that she had acquired a lower front dash panel from an earlier series 3 Bristol VRT. The design of the side lights is different and she wears a Bristol VR badge on the grille. From 1976 onwards, new deliveries of VRTs to the National Bus Company would no longer have this badge on the front grille because of NBC's desire to move away from the Bristol name. It also provided space for the new coloured NBC symbol to be applied on a small plate on the grille instead. Bristol VRTs ordered by other operators continued to have the Bristol VR badge right up to the type's demise in August 1981.

This sad sight was the aftermath of Bristol VRT 3070 (KOO 788V) being stolen from Chelmsford depot by a so-called joyrider, who crashed it just outside Chelmsford one night in the spring of 1994. Not surprisingly, it was withdrawn as a result of this incident.

Friday 29 April 1994 sees Leyland Lynx 1416 (F416 MWC) at All Saints Church, Maldon, looking quite smart as long as one overlooks the missing panel at the front offside of the bus.

Bristol VRT 3091 STW is seen on the 67A in West Mersea on 29 April 1994. The 67/67A was a replacement of the 7/7A.

Bristol VRT 3128 (XHK 233X) is seen in Colchester High Street, about to head down the B1022 to Maldon via Tipree, Great Totham and Heybridge on Friday 29 April 1994.

Bristol VRT 3078 (STW 22W) is seen in Colchester High Street on Friday 29 April 1994. This VR survived a long time with Eastern National, lasting until 2003 despite being withdrawn briefly and reinstated in 2002. This bus is believed to survive in Rotterdam in the Netherlands.

Seen in Chelmsford bus station when new in May 1994 is Denis Dart 812 (later to be renumbered 2812).

Leyland Lynx 1408 (F408 LTW) stands at Chelmsford bus station in May 1994. In the background can be seen a Class 321 Electric Multiple Unit (EMU) of the Great Eastern Train Operating Unit, as they were known at the time. This would have been on a service to London Liverpool Street. A Class 86 is propelling an Anglia Railways InterCity train from the rear, which would almost certainly be heading for Norwich. The 1993 Railways Act came into effect on 1 April 1994, abolishing the passenger business sectors of British Rail such as Network SouthEast and InterCity and replacing them with Train Operating Units, later to become franchises.

A Thamesway Dennis Dart with Plaxton Pointer bodywork is seen on the 214 LRT tendered route at London Liverpool Street on 15 July 1994. Badgerline certainly didn't pass up the opportunity to promote themselves as the parent company on the buses used on this prestigious route that ran right into the City of London.

Cityline Bristol VRT 5150 (AHW 201V) is seen in Chelmsford in June 1994. It was one of two Cityline VRTs that were loaned to Eastern National, with whom it was used at Colchester depot. This dual-door VRT with a four-speed fully automatic gearbox was arguably ill suited to the long inter-urban 53 between Colchester and Chelmsford. This bus is now preserved in NBC leaf green and white.

In November 1991, coach-seated Leyland Olympian 4013 (C413 HJN) is seen in autumn sunshine in Chelmsford town centre on the 36 to South Woodham Ferrers. This bus has now been repainted into the new Badgerline style livery. This bus was later transferred to First Devon & Cornwall, seeing further service at Plymouth depot.

Bristol VRT 3069 (KOO 787V) is seen at Heath Drive, Chelmsford, on a route normally worked by Mercedes 0709D minibuses, on a very dull 22 November 1994. This route's predecessor, the 44A/B, was worked by double-deckers from the mid-1950s up until 1991. This was due to EN bringing in drivers from elsewhere within the Badgerline Group to cover duties due to a severe driver shortage at the time, which was a result of EN dismissing a huge number of drivers during an industrial dispute. Due to regulations, the driver could only drive a full size bus.

Thamesway Dennis Dart (M925 TEV) is seen at Wood Street Tesco's, Chelmsford, on 18 January 1995. These new Darts had recently ousted elderly Leyland Nationals from Thamesway's share of the 152/3/4 group of routes between West Thurrock Lakeside and Chelmsford.

Also seen at Wood Street Tesco's on 18 January 1995 is Eastern National Leyland Lynx 1426 (F426 MJN), still in EN's deregulation livery of middle green and middle chrome yellow, often referred to by enthusiasts of the Essex transport scene as 'spinach and custard'.

Leyland Lynx 1408 (F408 LTW) is seen in Chelmsford bus station in April 1995. In the background can be seen a Class 312 EMU, which were the last multiple unit trains built by British Rail using the Mk 2 bodyshell, as well as being the last multiple units built with slam doors. They were the mainstay of outer suburban services on the Great Eastern Main Line for several years, the last ones being withdrawn in 2004.

Leyland Olympian coach 4501 (B691 BPU) is seen in the new livery on the newly introduced 71, which replaced the 53 between Chelmsford and Colchester in April of that year, the main difference being that the 71 left Chelmsford via Chelmer Village instead of going along Springfield Road. It is seen about to turn left from New London Road into Parkway in Chelmsford on Saturday 29 April 1995. This long-wheelbase Olympian was subsequently owned by Stephensons and Fargos.

Thamesway Dennis Dart 936 (M936 TEV) is seen on New London Road, Chelmsford, at the start of its lengthy journey to Lakeside on the 153 on Saturday 29 April 1995.

Also seen in New London Road, Chelmsford, on Saturday 29 April 1995 is Bristol VRT 3084 (STW 28W) on the 31 to Maldon.

Thamesway Dennis Dart 923 (M923 TEV) is seen at Chelmsford bus station on Saturday 29 April 1995. It was in April 1995 that the merger occurred between the Badgerline and GRT Groups to form FirstBus (now First).

Also taken on Saturday 29 April 1995 was this image of Leyland Tiger 1127 (A696 OHJ) with Alexander bodywork and still in the old livery. These dual-purpose vehicles were often used on inter-urban bus routes from Chelmsford, particularly the 31 to Maldon.

Leyland Lynx 1414 (F414 MNO) is seen on layover in Harlow bus station on 4 November 1995, waiting to return to its home town of Chelmsford. The blind appears to be set incorrectly as the route between Harlow and Chelmsford was the 59. Note the 'Welcome to FirstBus' window etching. These appeared in the late spring of 1995 on FirstBus fleets throughout Britain. This route is now operated by Arriva Herts & Essex from Harlow depot.

Bristol VRT 3092 (STW 36W) is seen at Witham Safeway (now Morrisons) on the 72 to Chelmsford on 10 February 1996. This was shortly after EN had a change of policy and the repainting of Bristol VRTs into the new livery had commenced.

New Dennis Dart/Plaxton 826 (N826 APU) is seen in Hatfield Peverel on 10 February 1996 on the now commercially operated 73 from Maldon to Chelmsford via Hatfield Peverel. This bus was delivered to Eastern National after the formation of FirstBus, hence the absence of a badger at the rear.

Mercedes 0609D 2642 (K642 GVX) is seen in Duke Street, Chelmsford, in March 1996. This was taken during the period when buses could be seen with both badgers at the rear and 'Welcome to FirstBus' etchings on their nearside window. It was around this time that First changed the legal name of their Essex acquisitions to Essex Buses.

Thamesway Leyland National YEV 326S is seen on a wet 6 July 1996 at Southend Central bus station. Although disliked among many transport enthusiasts, at least at first, the Leyland National proved to be a good, solid workhorse for Eastern National and Thamesway for many years.

Dennis Dart 829 (N829 APU) is seen when nearly new in Chelmsford bus station on 8 July 1996. Just visible on the edge of the photograph is one of the Leyland Tigers transferred to Eastern National for the 33/33X between Southend and Bishops Stortford via Chelmsford and Stansted Airport.

Three Bristol VRTs are seen at Harwich Town station on 8 July 1996: 3109 (UAR 599W) and the unidentified example behind it are in the new livery, while the bus in the background is still in the previous colour scheme. The plethora of fleet names on 3109 can leave no doubt as to which fleet it is a member of.

Leyland Olympian 4007 (C407 HJN) is just about to head off to Colchester on the 104 with the famous Harwich High Lighthouse acting as a backdrop on 8 July 1996.

Leyland National 1916 JHJ142V at Colchester bus station on 8 July 1996, not long after the iconic multi-storey car park above the bus stands had been demolished. I personally though this livery really suited the Leyland National.

Looking very smart on layover in Chelmsford bus station in the Badgerline style livery is Bristol VRT 3106 (UAR 596W), prior to heading off to Heybridge Basin on the 73 on 3 August 1996. This bus spent almost all of its life with EN at Chelmsford depot.

Seen at Maldon Promenade on Sunday 4 August 1996 is Leyland Olympian 4016 (C416 HJN). The badgers had been removed from the buses by this time.

Still in the ownership of FirstBus in 1996 was Bristol KSW (WNO 479), and on 13 October she made an appearance at the annual Canvey Island Bus Rally.

Also still owned by FirstBus was preserved Bristol K (AJN 825), which was new to Wescliff in 1939. This bus also made an appearance at Canvey Bus Rally in 1996.

Bristol K (AJN 825) looked superb in October 1996 at the Canvey Island Bus Rally. Unfortunately, she was very badly damaged in an arson attack the following winter and was lucky to survive. She has since been restored back to health and is once more seen at rallies.

Bristol VRT 3101 (UAR 591W) is wearing the new style of fleet name in the corporate style of FirstBus when seen at Colchester bus station on 24 January 1997.

1 May 1997 was a beautiful, sunny day and Thamesway Dennis Dart 903 (K903 CVW) looks very smart in the 'pink sash' livery as she passes the magnificent backdrop of St Pancras station on LRT route 214. Although this exterior wall of St Pancras has been largely untouched, just about everything else in this part of London has been completely transformed since this photograph was taken. The 214 has been temporarily withdrawn between Finsbury Square and Liverpool Street since 2012 due to Crossrail construction work.

Leyland Olympian 4008 (C408 HJN) is seen in Manningtree on 9 June 1997.

Leyland National 1921 (JHJ 147V), seen in Clacton-on-Sea on 9 June 1997. Although it was intended not to paint any Leyland Nationals into the new livery when it was introduced in 1993, EN had a change of mind and eventually quite a few received it.

Looking smart for a twelve-year-old bus, Leyland Olympian 4007 (C407 HJN) is photographed enjoying the late spring sunshine at a strangely deserted looking Colchester bus station on 9 June 1997 prior to heading off to Harwich on the 104.

Seen when about four months old, Dennis Lance 1503 (P503 MNO) is at Colchester bus station on 9 June 1997. The batch of thirteen buses to which 1503 belonged would be the last buses delivered in Eastern National livery.

Thamesway Dennis Dart 960 (N960 CPU) picks up passengers in Duke Street, Chelmsford, on 24 March 1998 on the 100 service to Lakeside, which had by this time replaced the 152 group of routes between Chelmsford and Lakeside. In keeping with FirstBus policy, the fleet name of the individual subsidiary has been relegated to small lettering on the side of the bus while the First fleet name has been given much more prominence.

By 24 March 1998, Leyland National 1916 (JHJ 142V) had received the new livery. By this time FirstBus had renamed itself FirstGroup to reflect its increasing interest in other forms of transport, particularly railway operations.

Brand-new Dennis Dart SLF 712 (R712 DJN) is seen at Southend bus station in FirstBus livery on 24 March 1998. It is route branded for the Diamond service to Bishops Stortford via Chelmsford and Stansted Airport, which was the successor to the 33/33X and the forerunner to the present X30 between Southend and Stansted Airport.

Also taken on 24 March 1998 is this image of Dennis Lance 1506 (P506 MNO) at Colchester. In keeping with the rest of the fleet, it has received smaller Eastern National fleet names and larger First names. It was a shame to see the EN name fading away, a process that was happening to several similar decades-long-established local operators through Britain at this time.

Bristol VRT 3083 (STW 27W) is seen at Chelmsford bus station on 24 March 1998.

Mercedes 0609D (K632 GVX) is seen in Gloucester Avenue, Chelmsford, on 15 August 1998 on the 45A to Moulsham Lodge Estate. The 45/45A was introduced in 1993 as the successor to the 44A/B between Chelmsford bus station and Moulsham Lodge.

Bristol VRT 3220 (WTH 949T) was an acquisition from sister company South Wales Transport in November 1990. It is seen here departing Colchester bus station on the 70 to Braintree on 1 September 1999.

Bristol VRT 3079 (STW 23W) stands at Colchester bus station on 1 September 1999. This VRT has been retrofitted with non-opening upper-deck front windows, which was quite common on surviving VRTs throughout Britain by this time, although it remained rare with Eastern National examples.

Bristol VRT 3101 departs Colchester bus station on the 66A to the pleasant riverside village of Rowhedge on 1 September 1999. It was a warm day, as can be seen by the fact that most of the window vents are open.

Also on 1 September 1999, Dennis Lance 1513 (P513 MNO) leaves Colchester bus station on the long journey to Harwich on the 104.

Another Lance working the 104 on 1 September 1999 was 1512 (P512 MNO). This batch of Lances were the only buses with Northern Counties bodywork ever delivered new to Eastern National.

No prizes for guessing the location of this image, despite the enigmatic destination display. This is mindful of when certain NBC companies often appeared to be heading to the mythical village of SERVICE back in the late 1970s/early 1980s. Mercedes 0709D J621 UTW is on Chelmsford town service 45A to Moulsham Lodge.

11 February 2000 sees Dennis Dart 2803 (L803 OPU) at Colchester bus station.

Also taken on 11 February 2000 was this picture of Bristol VRT 3079 (STW 23 W) at Wivenhoe. 3079 certainly didn't seem to be camera shy, as the various images of it in this book testify.

Mercedes 0709D 2634 (K634 GVX) is seen in Chelmsford town (now city) centre on 15 March 2000 on the crosstown 43 from North Melbourne to Oaklands Park. This route was a resurrection of the old 44, the number 43 having previously been used on a Writtle to Broomfield Hospital service (later extended to Halstead for a few years in the early 1990s). The Old Moulsham Estate, to which this bus was heading, has been served by several route numbers over the years, including the 35, the 46 and in recent years the 47.

Seen in Romford on 15 March 2000 is Leyland Lynx 1408 (F408 LTW), which has just arrived from Chelmsford on the 351. Just visible behind is a Stagecoach East London Volvo Olympian.

Dennis Lance 1501 (P501 MNO) is seen in Colchester bus station on 16 June 2000 wearing the new East Anglia livery recently introduced by First for its East Anglia operations. Predominantly yellow but with different coloured skirts for Eastern National, Thamesway and Eastern Counties, the idea was that this would make the vehicles easier to transfer between fleets.

New to West Yorkshire in 1981, Bristol VRT 3230 (SUB 789W) was one of several VRTs transferred from other Badgerline subsidiaries to EN following the fire at Colchester depot at Christmas 1994. It is seen here at the Canvey Island Bus Rally of 8 October 2000.

The last picture of the book taken in the twentieth century sees Bristol VRT 3112 (XHK 217X) at South Woodham railway station (now South Woodham Ferrers) on 20 October 2000. It is looking very good for a nineteen-year-old bus.

The first picture of the twenty-first century is First Eastern Counties Leyland Olympian 101 (XHK 235X), which was delivered new to Eastern National in 1981 as its 4000 and allocated to Southend. It is seen in Ipswich in March 2001. EN received three Olympians in 1981, and not long into their lives EN fitted them with VR-style upper-deck front windows. These passed to Thamesway in 1990 and were transferred later in life to Eastern Counties. As can be seen here, the upper-deck front window had been modified again by the time I took this photograph. It is a matter of regret that I managed to get just one photograph of a member of this batch while with EN or Thamesway, and the one I did take was of very poor quality.

Bristol VRT 3101 (UAR 591W) is seen in West Mersea on 3 May 2001. The front dash panel is looking very scruffy but the rest of the bus still looks smart for a twenty-year-old bus.

Leyland Lynx 1413 (F413 MNO), seen in May 2001 passing High Chelmer Shopping Centre in Chelmsford, is looking a little overdue for a repaint.

Mercedes-Benz 0709D 2672 (M672 VJN) is looking quite smart when seen in Chelmsford town centre in May 2001, although the EN name seems to be barely hanging on the side of the bus, well below eye level.

Seen outside the redevelopment of the former Bolinbrooke & Wenley store in Chelmsford town centre is Thamesway Dennis Dart (N969 CPU). Photographed in May 2001, it doesn't seem to be carrying a fleet number.

Leyland Lynx 1428 (F428 MJN) rests between duties in Chelmsford bus station in May 2001, accompanied by an Alexander-bodied Dart that had been transferred from Yorkshire Rider. This bus station closed in December 2004 and was replaced by a new development containing flats, shops and a smaller bus station.

One of the few vehicles delivered new in First livery but with EN fleet names is Dennis Dart SLF/Plaxton 731 (S731 TWC), which is also on layover at Chelmsford bus station. Behind is one of the remaining Bristol VRTs, which is now looking quite dated, next to the much newer Dennis Dart. Also visible in this picture is Arriva Dennis Dart K321 CVX, which is resting between turns on the Essex County Council contract route 32 to Ongar. The 32 used to be operated commercially by Eastern National, but the rural nature of the route made it unviable for commercial operation.

New to Yorkshire Rider is Alexander-bodied Dennis Dart M219 VWW. This bus was wearing First Leeds Citylink livery when transferred to First Eastern National. However, it is seen in the Eastern National version of the livery First had adopted for its East Anglia operations in May 2001.

14 August 2001 sees Mercedes 0709D 2674 (M674 VJN) having just arrived from Stansted Airport on an afternoon working of the 33. The 33 has had a chequered history, being the traditional route number to Great Dunmow, although it has at various times served Saffron Walden, Stansted Airport, Bishops Stortford and was, for a short while in the 1990s, extended south to Southend. The 33 was eventually withdrawn and replaced between Chelmsford and Stansted Airport by the 42A.

3079 did seem to like posing for my cameras over the years; however, this is the final image of it in this book, which was taken on 2 January 2002. By this time it was getting hard to find Bristol VRTs in service anywhere, although Colchester did seem to be one of the last strongholds for them. Captured in Colchester bus station, 2 January 2002, it would be withdrawn in September of that year and subsequently scrapped.

Also seen in Colchester bus station on 2 January 2002, having been transferred south from Yorkshire, is Volvo Olympian/Northern Counties L303 PWR.

Seen in the winter sunshine of 2 January 2002 is Dennis Dart 2829 (N829 APU).

Another picture taken in Colchester on 2 January 2002 sees Dennis Lance 1510 (P510 MNO) in the livery First used for step entrance buses. Unfortunately, the wet and muddy roads in North Essex had left their mark on 1510 that day.

Bristol VRT 3093 (STW 37W) is seen at West Mersea on 2 January 2002. New in February 1981, it would be withdrawn and scrapped in April 2002. It does look good for a bus just short of its twenty-first birthday, despite the efforts of the wet roads that day.

Leyland Lynx 1415 is seen in First livery and devoid of EN fleet names on 8 February 2002 at Stansted Airport bus station. This location would be a lot busier today.

On the morning of 12 April 2002 (twelve years to the day since Eastern National was taken over by Badgerline Holdings), Dennis Dart 2810 (L810 OPU) is seen traversing Chelmsford town centre on the busy cross-town service 45 from Writtle to Moulsham Lodge Estate.

Mercedes 0709D 2674 (M674 VJN) is seen turning off Springfield Park Lane onto Springfield Park Road on 20 April 2002. The blind is incorrectly set to Chelmer Village.

This is the third image of Leyland Lynx 1413 (F413 MNO) in this book, which has been seen in just as many liveries. Now in First livery, it is seen in Duke Street, Chelmsford, having just left the bus station embarking on the lengthy (and soon to be curtailed) 351 to Romford on 26 June 2002.

Alexander-bodied Dennis Dart 2911 (M229 VWW), new to Yorkshire Rider, is seen heading along Duke Street on the start of its very indirect route to Braintree via Chelmer Village, Boreham Village, Witham and Silver End. Although few people were expected to travel end to end on this route (although my late father once did), it did provide useful direct links. It is wearing the Eastern National version of the First East Anglia livery when seen on 26 June 2002.

A sneaky peak inside Chelmsford depot from Fairfield Road sees Bristol VRT 3072 (KOO 790V) still wearing Eastern National fleet names on 26 June 2002. This was destined to be the last surviving VRT in the First Essex fleet.

Still in Thamesway 'pink sash' livery and carrying route branding for the 100, although now devoid of anything other than First fleet names, Dennis Dart 967 (N967 CPU) is seen passing from Tindal Street to New London Road in Chelmsford town centre on 26 June 2002.

Although not of the greatest quality, I feel this photograph merits inclusion as it is the only photograph I took of a bus in the Thamesway version of First Group's East Anglia livery. Dennis Dart 948 (N948 CPU) is seen on London Road heading into Southend on the 27 on the last day of 2002.

I must admit to never loving this livery, but Dennis Lance 1503 (P503 MNO) does look smart when seen on Valentine's Day 2003 in Colchester bus station. It was common by this time to see pre-low-floor buses in various First Group fleets still in the local livery but without the local fleet name.

The days of Leyland Lynxes in the First Essex fleet were coming to an end by 2003, and on 24 July of that year 1419 (F419 MWC) is seen about to leave Victoria Circus, Southend, with a healthy load for a run along London Road to Basildon bus station. This bus was new to Eastern National in August 1988. It passed to Thamesway in 1990, was refurbished in 2001 and was withdrawn and sold for scrap in 2005. Out of the thirty Lynxes bought new by EN in 1988, just one is believed to survive, but I'd be more than happy to be corrected on that. The background to this photograph has changed tremendously since I took this photograph, with the roundabout having been replaced by a large traffic light-controlled T junction.

This photograph has some significance to me personally, as it was the last time I ever had a ride on a Bristol VRT in order to travel from A to B. 3072 (KOO 790V) is seen at Shenfield on Sunday 8 February 2004 having just arrived from Chelmsford on rail replacement work.

New to Eastern National while still in National Bus Company ownership as 4014, Leyland Olympian C414 HJN is seen in Chelmsford bus station in the summer of 2004 with its new fleet number, 34814. This was the number allocated to this Olympian as part of First's national renumbering scheme. This bus ended its days at the former Southern National depot in Weymouth.

We really are into the last vestiges of EN now. Dennis Dart L811 OPU was new to Eastern National as 811 under Badgerline ownership in the early 1990s and in the Badgerline style livery. Now devoid of the EN fleet name, but still wearing Eastern National colours, it is seen in Chelmsford in the spring of 2004. It is wearing both its EN fleet number of 2811 and the First national fleet number of 46811.

Seen at Braintree depot on the morning of 6 March 2004 is Bristol VRT 3072 (KOO 790V). As part of the First Essex Bristol VR farewell, 3072 and 3219 appeared on routes 72 and 351 on several Saturdays of early 2004. After this 3072 was kept on by First Essex in semi preservation until it was sold for preservation in 2010. This depot was closed and the land was sold soon after this photograph was taken, and First Essex opened a new depot in the Springwood Estate, although that has closed now as well.

As a nod to Eastern National's heritage, Dennis Dart 47252 (M450 UVV) was painted into an approximation of the Tilling Green livery worn by EN buses before the advent of National Bus Company leaf green. Although some people pointed out that the colour wasn't quite right, it was a nice touch to have traditional EN style depot and fleet number plates made. First, along with Stagecoach, have painted quite a few buses into the old liveries of the various bus operators they acquired over the years, although it has now been several years since a bus was painted into one of the old EN liveries. 47252 is seen in Duke Street, Chelmsford, while loading for Maldon opposite the site of the demolished bus station on 27 August 2005.

Semi-preserved Bristol VRT 3072 (KOO 790V), officially fleet number 38790, is seen at Takeley on a special duplicate run on the 33 on 3 July 2010.

This bus was the last vehicle in the First Essex fleet to carry the Eastern National fleet name and was sold for preservation in October 2010. Maybe one day First Essex will paint one of their current fleet members into one of the old Eastern National liveries. As before, this photograph was taken on 3 July 2010.